Leaving Santorini

poems by

Heather Corbally Bryant

Finishing Line Press
Georgetown, Kentucky

Leaving Santorini

ACKNOWLEDGMENTS

"Easter, Santorini," was previously published in *Compass Rose* (Georgetown:
Finishing Line Press, 2015)

"Ancient Thera," was previously published in *Compass Rose* (Georgetown:
Finishing Line Press, 2015)

"The Café," was previously published in *Thunderstorm* (Georgetown:
Finishing Line Press, 2017)

"Oia," was previously published in *Thunderstorm* (Georgetown: Finishing
Line Press, 2017)

Publisher: Leah Maines
Editor: Christen Kincaid
Cover Art: Thanks to Corrine Hansen Taylor
Author Photo: Richard Howard, Richard Howard Photgraphy,
www.richardhowardphotography.com

Cover Design: Elizabeth Maines McCleavy

Printed in the USA on acid-free paper.
Order online: www.finishinglinepress.com
also available on amazon.com

Author inquiries and mail orders:
Finishing Line Press
P. O. Box 1626
Georgetown, Kentucky 40324
U. S. A.

Table of Contents

Part III: Visiting Lissadell

for Lou

I *Easter Alone*

Topsy-Turvy

At times the world seems to tip, like a roller
Coaster, everything goes topsy-turvy on me,

Then, only then, I have to remember how to
Breathe—and just what it means to feel and

To be—how to live without those awful
Phone calls telling me in incremental detail

How my mother is dying—after a long bout of
Crying, I take a tub, gather myself up, and head

To the grocery store where I choose apples,
Clementines, tulips, peaches, and Easter

Chocolates, where I see people milling about,
Filling their carts—once more, and I feel alive.

My Mother's Jewelry

My mother spent her life in fear of losing things—
Not surprising for someone who moved ten times

Before she was in eleventh grade—she implores
Me to carry her jewelry home with me—don't

Check it—she whispers—it might be lost—ever
Since then, I've had a crick in my neck, a knotted

Place where I store my stress, my loneliness, my
Sorrow—until I can no longer open my mouth

Beyond a smidgeon—a physical therapist begins
To massage my strained muscles, to help me

Unclench my set jaw, to raise my shoulders high,
To keep my head up with pride for having walked

So long along a path burning with embers of
Desire, of disappointment, and of despair.

When Her Breath Left Her

I could feel the instant her breath left her—the
Moment her spirit passed, that word we choose
To use when we know someone will no longer

Last. I felt it, really, like in the movies, when her
Essence fled, leaving only the shred or carcass of
Her body, fascinating to me, comforting

That I was holding her; her nurse and I were
Just chatting on an ordinary Tuesday morning—
It was quick—she inhaled, paused, then her body

Stiffened, still warm with life, heavy with what
Had been—I lay with her body—her nurse told
Me I could stay as long as I needed and closed the

Door for privacy—I felt a reprieve from the
Gurgling, pumping, retrieving of oxygen pulsing
Through her, until I knew she was gone—

Her body ready to be turned to ash, hard to
Believe her remains could fit into a plain pine
Box on a chilly March morning when we stood

Beside to bless her body, receive her spirit.

Last Bills

Last wills and testaments, testimonials—isn't that the phrase?
Heirs gathered around a deathbed, as I wait for the letter

Appointing me executrix for my mother's worldly belongings,
A huge responsibility I bear, with no one to share to shepherd

Me through this unknown land, her death certificate no longer
Scares me, just a fancy blue piece of paper stamped with a seal

To make it official—it is the last bills that catch in my throat
When they arrive at my house—her last phone bill, through

To the end of the month, eight dollars and ten cents, her last
Monthly maintenance bill, pro rated by one day—a charge for

Extra oxygen, eight days before a diagnosis that would send her
Home, taking her on a journey she had no interest in completing.

The Minivan

I never pictured my mother's body being loaded
Into the back of a silver Honda Odyssey minivan—

Just like the one I used to own—in fact, I never pictured
My mother turning into a body at all—that was a

Secret I kept from myself—that she would die, like
Anyone else—I never pictured she would go—

That last morning when I held her so—it was to let
Her know, in the only way I could, that I understood

What she had been saying to me all those years, what
Was behind all those tears—and yet—once that impasse

Had been navigated, it was just me and her, down to
The very end; I kept my promise; I stayed with her,

I closed the gap that had been widening between
Us, festering for years; she did not die alone.

The Night My Mother Died

The night my mother died I had to telephone my former husband
To convey the news and to ask for his permission for her burial

In the plot we jointly owned, the only piece of property we had
Not discussed in our five-hour settlement meeting, barely averting

An ugly divorce trial; I was angry, raw from years of battling over
What we no longer had—and I was tired of pretending to be civil—

It was, after all, only eight months since we had sat in a stuffy
Lawyer's office dividing what I thought we had built together—

Grief made me furious—he wanted to come to her service; I
Forbade him; he refused to grant me rights to bury my mother

In said plot, necessitating a telephone call to my lawyer the following
Morning—what did you say—she asked? When I confessed, she told

Me I had to play nice—that was what was best—and so I've learned,
Over time, the hard way, to treat him just as someone I used to know.

Belongings

For so long my life has been scattered—
Here, there, and everywhere—I am ecstatic
To hear the movers from Boston have arrived
With their accents—joking about not dropping
The bureau drawers—at first I thought it would
Be strange to have her things near—now that
She is gone, but I was wrong—they bring me
Comfort, familiarity, a sense of continuity for
What has been but is still here somewhere—
In the clouds, the air, the dust, everywhere.

Easter, Alone

This is the first post-divorce holiday
I have spent entirely alone—and it is
Not nearly as bad as I have imagined—
In fact, the dog and I go for a walk—
Peaceful and light-hearted, that's how
I feel; it was my own Easter of serenity.

Conjugal Relations

I cannot even remember the last time we made
Love that summer when everything flew apart—

I recall the beach vacation where we slept miles
Away from each other though in the same bed.

Hard as I've tried, I cannot remember the last
Time we were together—you always complained

It was not how you wanted it to be, but then you
Would not say what you wanted—sometimes you

Smothered me, came dangerously close to killing
Me, at other times you begged me to stay so you

Could have a wife as well as a mistress
Or two or three—a family still you said we were—
No matter what; I cannot believe now what you

Really wanted to do—and how little of you I knew.

Restraining Order

If you hadn't told me lies
If you hadn't broken your vows,
If you had been a shred of
The self you pretended to be,
I would not have made you
Leave; the question I should
Have asked was not if, but when.

II   *Leaving Santorini*

Santorini Airport, Dusk

It is just past sunset when we land on this Cycladic
Island—I have been traveling for twenty-four hours
From central Pennsylvania to Philadelphia to

Zurich, to Athens, and now at last to this final
Destination—a volcanic island ringed by the
Aegean Sea, almost the southernmost land of

Greece—the light is fading apricot tinged with
Turquoise—I have been sitting next to a wedding
Dress, one that took up a whole seat—when I

Step off the plane, and walk down the
Narrow metal stairs I can see all around—
Warm air suffuses and surrounds me—for the

First time in a long while, I take in one long full
Breath of happiness as I walk towards a taxi.

Postcards

My son emails me—did I know I was on one of the most
Beautiful islands of earth? Santorini has popped up as

One of the ten most glorious sites on this planet—I can
Believe it, I write back—as I wake to yellow sunshine

Slicing the walls of the small house I've rented—when
I open the shutters, I see the azure bay brightening before me—

A whole new old world, one I've never explored before—
The colors are more pure than I can explain—everything

Tastes good again—after months of grief and hurt—a divorce
And a death within the same year—I'm healing, I can tell—

I no longer feel as though I am falling, falling through
The earth—at night, I can see Venus beginning to rise.

First Rain

The first time it rains, drops begins to splatter
Across the windshield of the taxi I'm taking to Fira
To explore the shopping—I've been on this island

For almost a week without getting into a car—I've
Hiked or swum almost everywhere—but beneath
The gray morning skies I decide to take a ride

To see what I can see, a British couple joins me,
Talking of where they might be able to find a cup
Of tea—they ask me to join them, but I would

Rather be alone—the shop I find sells
Everything in white—the owner asks me what
Cruise ship I'm on—I tell her I'm here on my

Own—I buy a sweater to warm the way home.

Amoudi Bay

Nothing on this island is exactly how I have imagined
It would be and yet, in another way, it is exactly how
I have pictured it—the beaches are covered with craggy

Black rocks—I am intrepid, climbing down over three
Hundred steep steps from the small village of Oia—I
Carry a backpack with a picnic—and when I get to

A smooth spot hidden in the rocks, I pull off my shirt
And shorts, jump in and then push off—this Aegean
Sea is glorious, if a bit chilly this May—I make my

Way all around a tiny rocky island—until I find black sand.

Red Springs

I leap off the boat into the red water, sulfuric
Sand soft beneath my feet—burbling hot springs—
I turn red all over, covered with goopy and

Gritty mud from Volcanic springs—I float
On my back in bubbling water, arms spread wide,
Buoyant with the clarity of gravity and grace—

Only bright blue skies and a few puffy clouds.

Skala

I eat at this restaurant at least three times,
Maybe four—it becomes my local, my favorite—

I am the last guest to be seated on Greek Easter;
I devour my favorite foods: fava and salad with

Olives and feta, lamb and Moussaka; I sample
Yet another volcanic wine from the shrubs

That do not resemble vineyards—the land here
Is difficult to cultivate, seemingly impossible—

White flowing wine nothing short of miraculous.

Captain Alphonso Cave House

I luxuriate in not rushing in the shower, flushed
Cheeks under hot water, water flowing down

All over my nakedness—and I feel sensual in
A way I would not have ever guessed, running

My fingers along my body—
Periwinkle clay walls soft, my hair long now

Curling, water steaming, I close my eyes and
Think about how far away I am from everything

I know—on an island across the world from
Where I usually live, freer than I've ever been.

Easter, Santorini

Propelled by the crowds, I follow a wave of people
Towards the church square; it is beautiful there—
A blue dome luminescent, rising to the sky

And I see candles blessed and lit, shouts, commotions,
A fight—fireworks everywhere—faces illuminate,
Sparklers tossed in the air, "big bombs coming,"

A grandfather warns, we are all swept along with
Passion arising—a bit fearful, I climb some stairs
To watch the crowd below celebrating the glory and

The resurrection—walking back, I pass Greek lilies
In bloom—gunpowder lingers in the air amidst
Sweet blossoms, may our world last forever, Amen.

Songs of the Cyclades

The songs of the Cyclades have long called to me, ever since I read of Homer's alluring sweet nymphs and open seas—the idea of Poseidon's wrath falling

Upon these perpetually seductive nymphs who used their secret powers to make Odysseus tarry long while he should have been making his way home—

Until Poseidon grew so angry that he turned them all to stone—creating a circular sea of sacred islands out of these volcanic eruptions so they could stay in the rocks

For eternity—calling out only in land formation what they would trade for love—embracing the land itself with their sound properties—I would love nothing better than to

Sleep in these magical rocks, these dots in the Aegean Sea with their blue and green miracles speckled throughout the turquoise sea—unlike any other water I have ever

Seen, these islands have always fascinated me with their circular worship to the God of the sea—placed around a circle of the sacred, like Stonehenge, another place of stone set

In earth for worship—even their translated names call to me: Andros, Timos, Keas, the bare hills of Mykonos, Santorini where divers once searched for the mythical city of

Atlantis, Kythonos, Anafi, Ios, or violet in English where Homer's mother is said to have been born—and the original poet buried there—amidst a field of violets—Folegandes,

Unspoiled by tourism, the son of Minos, the retreat of Seritos, the leaving of this world for another—Kiniolos, western harsh volcanic edge—Sitnos, Sikinos, of

Steep terraces and white chapels heading down to the hills—Delos, birth Place of Apollos and Artemis—Paros with its shimmering heat and Byzantine footpaths—these

Names call out to me—Naxos—the biggest and greenest of all, Traklia, Schinoussa, a tiny tenacious group of islands linked together by a narrow strait—the edges

Of the land narrowing and twirling and spinning away from the strand of human understanding—that farthest edge where water meets shore and then breaks again—

Donousa, Antiparos, Amorges—big and blue, here is where the blue is bluer than the bluest blue could ever hope to be, the unmistakable blueness of the Aegean Sea.

Betrayal

I remember once watching a play where
A husband commits adultery; my one thought:
I know I cannot stand that happening to me.

So it was with assurance that I closed my eyes
And chose the man who said he would always
Love me, *love always* was how he signed

Every card, for every occasion, love always,
He quoted e.e. Cummings, *I carry your heart
In my heart*, and indeed he did, until he broke

The whole marriage into pieces with one
Sidelong remark—we are not where he wanted
To be after fifteen years of matrimony—that was

My first sign that all was not as it seemed—he
Begged for forgiveness and I offered what I
Could, but it was not enough, nothing was

Ever enough for him; so I learned the hard
Way that he would go right ahead and grind
My heart into the pavement every chance he got.

Silver Anniversary

A British man and I end up on the same beach,
Having both swum a bit past our reach—before
We take the plunge back into the May Sea, he asks

Me what occasion I am celebrating on my
Vacation—he and his wife are there for their
Silver, a word he says with pleasure—and I

Realize on my frigid swim along the shoreline
That I am here celebrating the end of my marriage,
The prison where I needed to sleep, eat, and

Answer every command as if it were a demand,
Nothing ever according to my own desires—it
Was always someone else I had to please—I do

The math in my head—I made it through almost
Twenty-three years of turmoil and despair, until
I understood the ruin that had become our love.

Our divorce decree came through two weeks
Short of what would have been our silver
Anniversary—there is sorrow for what could

Have been, there is also great joy in knowing
I have freed myself from the tyrant who would
Not have ever let go of me, but yet saw nothing

Wrong with falling into the arms of whatever
Woman happened to catch his fancy next—it
Didn't matter why, as I have at last learned,

Only that he would never be able to love me.

Ancient Thera

How did these ancient people carry such heavy loads?
For such long distances, that's what I want to know—

And how did they carve such delicate patterns and
Designs into thick rocks—how did they balance

A statue of Aphrodite on this rectangular pedestal—
On this spit of land, cliff jutting out into the Mediterranean

Sea—stone carvers must learn, practice, and perfect
Their art, like any other—maybe it should come as no

Surprise that they fashioned these shapes—three days
After my visit to the ruins, the man who is carving my

Mother's stone calls me, just to double check her dates,
Hard to believe she's been gone eight months, that she

Lived almost to the end of her eighth decade—I like to
Remember her story of visiting Greek ruins with my father.

Donkeys

One morning I realize why I feel as though I'm in a movie—
Because I have seen the scene before me on the big screen;

Jingling bells wake me everyday—the sound of donkeys
Being led to the steep stairs at the end of the island—the

Stairs where they lug heavy tourists up and down more
Times than I can count—by dusk, the donkeys pass by

My windows again, this time they are tired, worn, thirsty—
And I am sorry for their lot—when their owners hit them

With whips to make them go faster, I have to look away.

Hiking to Fira

Sunday afternoon, a sultry island day: sunshine pours heavy,
Sweat clings to my forehead, just sitting outside reading
Under a white umbrella makes me perspire; I delay

Packing for the trek to Fira: eventually, I select water,
Camera, sunscreen, a watch but no map, the sign is easy to see—
I cannot possibly miss it on my way out of Oia, or

So Maria says. I start my dusty walk along the switchback road
For at least a mile; early on I spot specks of people crossing
By a church on high, I want to get to where they are. I

Take a sharp right upward turn scrambling uphill where I only see
The remains of a house started, foundation half poured, haphazard
Rocks set in unlikely places. I wonder if I can reach the path from

Here just by digging my feet into the mountain; a passerby brings
A voice of reason, the trail will be difficult to catch, besides it is very
Steep and I am carrying a heavy backpack, after all.

Dejected, I turn around, and take pictures of the vistas from a
Scenic lookout as if to say this venture today has not been in vain
After all; not at all, a few turns later I spot a sign, crooked,

Facing backwards, almost illegible, mysterious like so much else
In Greece—I decide to give it a try, spending hours climbing
The ridge until I can see both sides of Santorini, as promised;

I pass rocky cliffs, cement chains of houses begun, abandoned
Apparently in haste, resorts with tempting pools, a blue dome
Where I almost make another wrong turn until I glance to

My left and see the white town of Fira rising in the distance
At almost the most beautiful hour with rose-tinged light splashing
On the Mediterranean ocean below; I slow my pace; I've been

Walking fast, and I'm thirsty now, parched you might say.
I stop to gaze down the four hundred steps I've descended
Once before, the harbor where the yacht is still docked; I tumble

Into a taxi for the ride back, ecstatic to have found what I was
Looking for, the journey made sweeter by my earlier impasse.

Perisa Beach

The sand here is black, all black—
I place a towel beneath me and

Lie down to tan—I don't mind
Being alone here—eventually I

Walk into the water and swim
Back and forth, parallel to shore—

Always keeping the horizon line
In clear sight—I lose count of

The laps—when I leave the
Water, I realize I am shivering—

It is late May here, still spring.

The Cafe

Everyday I came to this cafe, every morning, first thing, when the
Light awakened me I walked down the cobbled streets, keeping out
Of the donkeys' way—first thing, I came to this place and drank

One cappuccino—sometimes two—and I felt everything again, as if for the first
Time—I could see all the way to the horizon's line, I could feel my
World righting itself again—I stopped waking feeling as though I

Were falling, falling through everything until there was nowhere left to fall—on
This magical island I began to believe I could live again in beauty and in peace,
As though I could imagine a new universe where there was more

Sunshine and less grief—each morning, the proprietor brought me two pastries
With my drink—everyday we greeted one another with grins; when I put my
Coins on the counter, he wished me good day, and on my very

Last morning he waived the receipt away and wished me Godspeed on my trip
Home to England—I pretended that's where I lived—in our two weeks, we had
Learned so little about one another and yet, if I saw him
Tomorrow, I would know to smile at him.

Second Rain

The second rain comes on my penultimate
Afternoon here—the trip is coming to an

End—the dark clouds match my mood—
I don't ever want to leave this place, even

In the rain—I know part of why it is my
Paradise is because I have discovered it

All on my own—and it is also better than
I have imagined—Walker Percy explained

The phenomenon of the difficulty of seeing
Something as if for the first time—and yet,

This island has become my Eden, for now.

Coral Veritable

One of the last things my father gave me
Was a tiny bottle of miniature pieces of

Coral that he brought back from Greece,
Coral Veritable stamped in gold letters on

The label circling the front of this treasure—
That and the matching coral earrings I've since

Lost—I remember his spiky black handwriting
On the card—he'd written *your tummy will never*

Outgrow these—a perfect note given I'd just told him I
Was expecting twins, a fact he marveled over—

I've kept that tiny bottle with me as a talisman
Of his spirit of adventure—indomitable as I

Now hope to be—I keep this last remnant with me.

Oia

Sometimes it is difficult to find a place of peace in our restless world; sometimes
It is hard to stop the noise from coming in, the ceaseless notifications of this
Or of that—sometimes it is almost impossible just to be—apparently, it keeps
Becoming more difficult to be quiet, relaxed—maybe when people

Sought healing in quiet streams or sweet springs they found just that—even
When they were riding along in bumpy Surrey buggies or horses or climbing
Mountains looking for views—maybe they knew something we did not—to

Take the time to look at what is right in front of you, right before your very
Eyes.

The Caldera

I will never tire of this view—the steep island
Cliff giving way to the tranquil bay—the

Caldera as it's called—hard to believe that
Long ago a volcano blew up this whole piece

Of earth—breaking the chain of land, leaving
Remnants of its fiery explosion at the

Bottom of this circle of water that has become
My world, the place where I remember what is left.

Last Night

I sip whiskey before the sunset, after a day
In the car exploring beaches, ruins, and

Desolate resorts, like Florida in the off
Season, umbrellas being dragged across

The black sand—I think I am beginning
To understand this place—even though

I cannot speak a word of language—
Coltrane plays in the background—

Dusk begins to settle, the sun a tangerine
Glow low in the sky—I don't want to go.

Leaving Santorini

When I get up to leave, it is five in the morning—still
Dark—a man comes to help me gather my belongings—

We walk all the way through town to the waiting taxi—
He hugs me goodbye—we have become friends in our

Time here—he showed me where to get the best wifi,
How to rent a car, how to find a catamaran, how to

Make the toilets work, a delicate task—and he wishes
Me well on my way home—as the taxi pulls away

On that dusty early morning, I think of the journey
Ahead—first to the airport, then through customs

And a small plane over the Caldera, this time at
Dawn and it is impossible to be in Greece for long

Without thinking of Homer and his rosy-fingered
Dawn—the same dawn I witness as the plane

Ascends on its way to the mainland—the attendants
Come through with coffee which tastes bitter

Compared to the lattes I have come to love at
The café—when I land in Athens I have enough

Time to stare out the windows at the parched
Land, to watch the bustle of passengers arriving

And departing—conscious of time again, I buy
A Swatch at a small shop—determined to make

These last hours last—the customs agent who
Stamps my passport asks me if I have enjoyed

My stay—yes, I nod, yes, very much, I say—
And then I am off, to Zurich, retracing my

Steps—since the last time I was here a
Lifetime has passed—in Switzerland, I

Check my email again—coming back to
The world of obligations I have left

Behind—I sleep for much of the long
Way back across the Atlantic—and when

We land in Philadelphia, the passengers
Clap—I manage to exit security and walk

Miles or so it seems back to clearance—I
Claim my luggage and pass through US

Border Control after two hours in line—
A dog sniffs me; I say I have no cheese,

No fresh goods, and no I have not been
To any farms; I don't say that I have

Swum in volcanic springs, that I've
Seen the world in a grain of coral,

That I've watched sunset over
The Caldera thirteen times, minus

One night when it was raining.

Wildcard

I am a wildcard—I have come to recognize the
Fly fishers tossing lines out into thin air—married

Men interested in a divorcée—just friends they
Say, as they message me their cell phone

Numbers, the nights they will be staying in
Hotels—and I want to know if their wives

Are already asleep in another room, in a different
State—are they talking to women like me,

Women they have not seen in decades—but
Suddenly recalled and then I feel a need to

Be clean, to be free, to be clear—I send a note
To my first lover saying I am sorry, because

I think I kind of broke his heart—I was too
Young, too foolish, looking for all the wrong

Qualities—no need, he says, and besides we
Had a wonderful time together—I am so glad

To hear that, because we did have a lot of
Laughs—he is Italian, warm, and funny—

I tell him I write poetry now and he looks it
All up—all of it—and wants copies of my

Books—it is then I realize I am emerging—
He says he loves my words that I sound just

Like I did back in the day—that is exactly
What I could have hoped he would say, but I

Did not dare to hope those would be

The words he might say to me, even though
He is not free, I hope one day he might be.

One Hundred Miles from Boston

The captain announces we are on our initial descent to Boston—
I will never forget the moment I arrived in Santorini and realized

I was free—now I carry that knowledge with me, a talisman
Of memory—shortly after that trip—just three months later, I

Learned I would be coming home again, home to the rocky
Shore of New England and all that was waiting there for me—

Late at night now, flying up the shoreline, I remember all over
Again what it is like to call Boston home—I will never forget

How far away I traveled, how many obstacles were placed in
My way, both by others and of my own making—how far I felt

From the windswept ocean—and now I know what it means to
Call a place home, and how sometimes the only way to know

What home means is to leave it—and are there only two stories
Really, the one of the stranger coming into town, and the one

Of the villager adventuring, the *Iliad* and the *Odyssey*, and now
Neither my mother or father is here, but a new life awaits me,

A new story waiting to unspool, a story of reunion, remembering,
And blessing, just as Odysseus knew Argos, I know where I

Belong—the flight attendants prepare the cabin for arrival, we
Are asked to power down our devices—the blinking screen

Goes blank, I look out the window and see the amber lights
Hugging the shoreline, black waters alongside them—and I

Think about what it will be like to touch down on the runway
Besides the ocean, and what it is like to have all my belongings

With me again, to have brought coherence to my life, to have

Learned that no one else can save me, no one here on earth.

Santorini showed me what was waiting here for us; I will
Return to that airport when the rosy dusk of apricot

Descends, and I will see it again, as if for the first time.

Part III   *Visiting Lissadell*

Welcome to Ireland

Dublin airport at five thirty in the morning—pitch-black darkness
Of winter, a bush of pink roses blooming, a tub of heather, Santa
Claus on skis in the terminal—three people are waiting for the bus—

It is that traveler's in between time—no time really and a young man
Comes along, still drunk—beer frozen in his beard—a gift shop tooth
Brush sticking out of his pocket, looking for 300 quid to settle his bet

On an unfortunate ticket to Mallorca—"Welcome to Ireland," the elderly
Man says with bitterness when the bus driver refuses his credit card.

The Traffic Warden

The bus bumped the whole way—beginning in the dark rain
Through Dublin's outskirts in the midst of morning commute—
All the way along the northern route, heading west in Ireland—

Nowhere to go to the east, starting on Ireland's easternmost tip,
All that way through villages, market towns, and beyond in
Enniskillen—we stopped in the north when not too long ago

Guards would have accompanied us to make sure we didn't digress—
Here it was just another village—I sleep and wake and doze as we pass
Fields and rows of hedges—oak trees planted on estates—sunshine

Surprises me in Ballyshannon where Michael Whelan, a traffic
Warden, comes to my aid, Driving me to fetch my bag in Kinlouch,
And then back to Bundoran, only out of the niceness

Of his heart—no more. No less, and I remain in awe of his kindness.

Rougey Cliff Walk

Do not approach the cliff edge.

A balmy day, stiff winds they say,
A euphemism for what cannot be—

Described as anything other than
Cruel cold, the wind against us—

Flying against us, the wind at my
Back—mountains really do—

Turn to clouds here, across the
Way—sun-topped cliffs away—

On the other side of Donegal Bay,
When I turn around and look

West all I see is the seaside
Town bundled up for winter, pink

Painted houses made ready for
The cold—it is difficult to

Imagine warmth suffusing in this place.

Snow

In one day it snows, sleets, rains, and mists—
And is generally damper than I can imagine

Feeling—no wonder people drink tea by the
Pot-full, one cup is not enough to stay warm—

Once you get cold, it's the kind of chill that takes
Forever to ease, once you're chilled, only a cup

Of tea and a hot whiskey will have a chance of
Keeping you on your toes—and I think of the

Last line of "The Dead,"—the snow is *falling*
Faintly, faintly falling all over Ireland.

Guinness Rounds at the Pub

It has been years since I have drunk this much—
But as long as he is willing to buy us all rounds,

We succumb until the pub spins and I think of
The world and how small it can be—and also how

Big, but it seems tiny in this night in Bundoran
When we are all sitting here together, gathered round,

Warmed with whiskey and words tying us all
Together, huddled around a table in Bundoran.

Visiting Lissadell

Instantly my toes feel the damp; it climbs up my legs, I have
Literally caught a chill running from the bottom of my feet up to my
Forehead—seventy-four rooms heated only by fireplaces—the stone

Is massive in its coldness—the front hallway crafted entirely
Of Kilkenny marble, carted here by crews of thousands, hewed out of
The ground—the beautiful here is too beautiful to say—the ground is

Sweeping down to the waters and mountains beyond—the scene that
Yeats immortalized when he visited the Gore-Booth sisters and wrote
About their silk kimonos, like gazelles they were—sitting by the

Windows waiting for the world—one room was all for Eva, her private
Sitting room where drinks would be served, where she would not have
Brought a gun, instead where she sat and etched her name in

The glass pane, scratching out the letters with a large-cut diamond.

The Billiard Room

The guide closes the door, shutting out the fire so the visitors can
Hear his southern drawl, incongruous here—I make a list of what he
Is saying—I don't want to forget anything—I have been waiting to come

Here for years—it is at once how I thought it be and also entirely different—the
House is much bigger than I could grasp or fathom, even imagine—the life
Large and grand—the billiard table sits in the center of the room, a scoring
Tablet

Built into the wall, still set with the results of the last game played,
As though time has stopped again—here everything is preserved,
I peer into a cabinet lined with leather books to spot among the artifacts

A pheasant egg, and perhaps a quail—across the way an articulate whale that
An ancestor speared, and a stuffed preserved pheasant, an atlas to spin the
World, here a respositing of the universe in a corner of

Kilkenny—a world preserved, known and unknown, for any visitor to see.

The Kitchen

Beneath the cavernous dining room, we wind down a narrow stair to the
Kitchen where the work was done—it's here I feel the dampness the
Most acutely—walls dug beneath the earth, windows to peek above at

The rain as it must have swept through the valley, though the stonewalls
Are thick, they must keep the cold in—bottles and cutlery are scattered,
A bottle of gripe water, a woman says it must come from the North,

You can't get it here anymore—contains alcohol, you see, to rub along a
Fussy baby's teething gums—the wooden table has sunken parts, indents
From centuries of cooks placing hot pots down in the midst of cooking for

A crowd—it is hard to imagine food being prepared here—and then placed
In the dumbwaiter for the guests waiting upstairs—who were waiting,
Perhaps not so patiently, for their delicacies—in any one week there could

Be three hundred rats running free—a shilling prize for the highest kill.

A Dinner Party

After arriving by carriage, gas lighting the avenues—gas
Mined beneath the acres of the estate—guests would arrive in the
Portico where the butler would meet them and escort them inside—

Eventually, they would pass through the entrance way and into the
Grand gallery where the gasolier would have been illuminated for
The occasion—the organ might be playing and drinks passed around—

And all would be filled with noise and laughter and sound—and who
Would have been thinking of what might be happening underground,
Beneath the earth the conquerors surveyed—who might have been

Thinking of the hundreds of people laboring to make one festive evening?

The Bear

Long windows line this room and I imagine Yeats sitting here, making
His case for one daughter or another, he spent so much of his life
Looking for a wife—and was it the chase for him? I wonder what he

Would have thought as he looked out at what I still see—the scene
Stiller in front of us—portraits of course, but someone painted a dog
On one of the columns, something for everyone really—and just beside

The head of the table, so close I might have jumped, a full-size stuffed
Bear, brought back from Finland in 1880, just standing there, as though
Entirely alive—and is it not the past speaking to us?

The Tunnel

Here is where I stand: outside Lissadell House in the servants'
Courtyard where they could go outside to get a bit of air, where
They came to work every morning, beside where the coachmen

Slept in their clothes in case they were needed for a night time
Emergency ride, kept at the beck and call of the owner of the
Hall—beside the room where the safe was kept for depositing

Their rent—and as I stand looking up the tunnel I see the ground
Closing in, and for the first time the chill comes through—
It dawns on me just how difficult this life would be—what it might

Be like to walk down that darkening tunnel every morning of your life.

Bealach Atlantaigh, Wild Atlantic Way

The Wild Atlantic way has earned its name—wind rips against me
As I round the Rougey cliffs—it is impossible to stand upright as I look
Across to the other side, topped with snow and wind, everywhere

Wind—the seas churn, the seas of the North Atlantic in January—
And I see there is no place for the faint or timid—all those who left,
Including my maternal ancestors, had to face the wild Atlantic,

That is what was standing between them and America, between
Famine, the potato blight, and what it might take to change a life—
And how difficult it might have been to leave are the details that

Chafe my heart, a quaint wooden cross marking a life lost to sea.

Sanderlings

Here are the sea birds of Bundoran: sanderlings,
Mute swan, great black-backed gull, cormorant,
Oystercatcher, grey plover, ringed plover, Brent

Goose, grey heron, scoter, turnstone, purple sand-
Piper, shown aloft, also greenshank, common
Sandpiper, dipper dunlin, curlew, eider duck,

Redshank, herring gull, and black-headed gull—
All those identified as a sign for us to see—but
First, a mute swan flying right towards me—sign

Posted by St. Marcarten save the wildlife group.

A Missing Sea Buoy

Along the rugged cliffs, there is nothing to be missed—sea
And sand and surf, nothing kept us from the sea, but one
Missstep, one missed step, and we would tumble down—we

Would not be the first to drown—the language is harsh—a
Yellow sea—buoys are kept in boxes along the coastline—we
Are warned, *A missing sea buoy equals a missing life*, and all the

Boxes I pass are full, save for one, and I wonder, is that the one
Where the life was lost, is that the one that necessitated the
Cross, is that the place where human and sea crossed, and

A life was lost, perhaps drowned at sea, certainly gone.

The Eight a.m. Bus to Dublin

We have a tough time making this bus Sunday morning—
Darkness stays long here—halfway through the year,
The night lingers in the morning—and we are all in that

Space of travel, that place between here and there, where we
Have to scatter from this tiny village of grass and sea where
We have been in another world—the smell of diesel creeps

Through the bus as the driver presses the accelerator, we
Leave the curving crossroads of the west, traveling first to
The north, then eastwards, through the estates where England

Conquered, to Dublin, the river Liffey flowing through the city.

St. Patrick's Cathedral on Martin Luther King Day

I don't believe in anything I can name: word, spirit, god, or deity,
Rather I live free from organized belief but sometimes I am caught
Inside something far larger than anything I can describe—as is so

In Dublin town when I walk across the city to step inside St. Patrick's
Cathedral, a private anniversary for me—knowing that, on this day,
Twenty-two years ago, my life was saved—no one ever told me the

Exact details but I'm pretty sure it was not looking good for
Awhile that January afternoon—and in that same moment I gave birth
To two lives who amazed me and set me free in their remarkableness—

In this quiet moment beneath the blue and yellow stained glass window,
Beside an ancient stone baptismal font, I whisper the Lord's Prayer, the
Only one I know—my mother told me to memorize it because it might

Come in handy sometime—I give thanks for having been allowed to stay.

Hyacinths Blooming on Dame Street

Even though the damp is piercing through me—and it
Still rains off and on almost continuously—the hyacinths
Are blooming on Dame Street—pink hyacinths sprout,

Forcing their shoots out of the earth, beside them primroses
Blue, yellow, and sweet—even in January the
Bulbs are sprouting—I remember the pink roses I saw

Blooming at five in the morning on the first morning
I landed in Ireland—beside the bus stop at the airport—
Every time I arrive here, I feel at home—more each time

I think of the hyacinth girl coming back from the garden.

Traffic Calming

A sign points simply to "The West," with an arrow pointing
Towards a blue wave, a sign leads to tra, the beach, carraig
Means rock, margadh means market, neamh means heaven,

The road to Sligo is marked, on the way to Yeats's grave,
Under Ben Bulben, Kilkenny, cill means church, the poison
Glen was where the Cyclops fought but it might have been

Misspelled as in might have been meant to be called heaven
Instead, as the road slows and narrows, the sign suggests
"Traffic calming" ahead—before the night begins, and with
It the fiddles and the craic, when the warm Guinness is poured.

Sunday Afternoon at the Castle Hotel

Sunday afternoon I pull the curtains
On this damp day—in my universe it
Is warm and I take a deep bath, luxuriating
In the hot water—and bubbles—I brew
Some tea—and all is cozy and sweet—
Remembrance and recovery, I am me again.

The New World

And to think that they called this the new world, when the Spaniards
Came and mixed their brown eyes and darker skin with the pale faced
Locals—it was a new world then, to them, but when you look at the

Rocks, the peat, the ledges, the islands, only then do you realize
It was all here before, all of it, and nothing more, it is the oldest world,
Not the new—the hydrangea here bloom magenta; something about

The soil, the rock, the harsh unyielding land under the shadow of
Mountain and clouds—of all the places in the world, this is where I
Might like to be buried, where the shadows cross the land, under

Ben Bulben, the mountain Yeats chose for his final resting place, the
Mountain he memorialized, near the bogs where the peat grew over
The dead who were long left, where the bog people also came to rest.

Writer's Museum

I can see this place from my hotel and, when I
Enter the doors I can't even remember if I've
Ever been here before—I don't think so—but
Then so much of what happened before I do not
Remember—I am here now, that's what
Matters and I am seeing everything as if for the
First time; there right in front of me, I encounter
Elizabeth Bowen, looking right back at me.

Old Reading Room at the Marsh Library

In St. Patrick's close, behind the cathedral, hidden in shadow
Is the oldest public library in Ireland, dating from 1707 when
The rarest books had to be read in cages, lest they be stolen;
The librarian locked the scholars in—and they were only men—
Men who were considered worthy of being able to apprehend
The books—the door is close to hidden when I spy the number
On a January noontime that is almost dark, blackened clouds and
Wind—yet behind lies the illumination of the ages, at least the
Old ages, often the middle ages—and at long last, I touch the table
Where Joyce used to read, where he based, scholars say, the
Proteus episode of *Ulysses*, when his protagonist, Stephen Dedalus
Walked the "Stagnant bay" of Marsh's library, also where Stephen
Read the fading prophecies of Joachim Abbas.

Island Dream Songs

Something about the way water laps the shore,
The way the boat slips into a dock, the plane
Finds a runway on a narrow slit of land—

Something about islands captivates me—
It's not the feeling of being a prisoner,
Rather the setting free—the remoter the

Better—the sense of escape, of tranquility,
Of being away from the world, close to
Eternity—the way water circles land,

Reminding us of the simplicity and clarity
Of being alone on an island—no man is
An island—no woman either—yet, I

Want to remember this, all of this, as I
Close my eyes just before the last descent.

Heather Corbally Bryant (formerly Heather Bryant Jordan) teaches in the Writing Program at Wellesley College. Previously, she taught at the Pennsylvania State University, the University of Michigan, and Harvard College where she won awards for her teaching. She received her A.B. with honors in History and Literature from Harvard where she received the Boston Ruskin Prize for her thesis. She received her PhD in Modern British and Irish Literature from the University of Michigan where she was a Regents Fellow.

Her academic publications include, *How Will the Heart Endure: Elizabeth Bowen* and *the Landscape of War* (University of Michigan Press, 1992) which received the Donald Murphy Prize for best first book. She assisted in the research for the Cornell Yeats Series, and has published academic articles in *Review, Text, The New Hibernia Review, The Library Chronicle of the University of Texas at Austin* among others. She has given papers and readings at international conferences, bookstores, and universities.

Beyond her academic publications, Heather Corbally Bryant has published a work of creative nonfiction, *You Can't Wrap Fire in Paper* (Ardent Writer Press, 2018) as well as seven books of poetry: *Cheap Grace* (Finishing Line Press, 2011), *Lottery Ticket* (The Parallel Press Series of the University of Wisconsin, Madison, 2013), *Compass Rose* (Finishing Line Press, 2015), *My Wedding Dress* (Finishing Line Press, 2016), *Thunderstorm* (Finishing Line Press, 2017), *Eve's Lament* (Finishing Line Press, 2018) and *James Joyce's Water Closet*, which won honorable mention in the 2017 Open Chapbook Competition of Finishing Line Press. *Thunderstorm* was nominated for a 2018 Massachusetts Book Award, and her poetry has also been nominated for a Pushcart Prize. Her ninth book of poetry, *Practicing Yoga in a Former Shoe Factory*, will be published by Finishing Line Press in the spring of 2020.

Heathercorballybryant.com

www.ingramcontent.com/pod-product-compliance
Lightning Source LLC
Chambersburg PA
CBHW021156090426
42740CB00008B/1119